CW01456660

Eight Billionaire Strategies for Breakthrough Stock Market Success

Tim Bost

Harmonic Research Associates
Sarasota, Florida, USA

**Eight Billionaire Strategies
for Breakthrough Stock Market Success**

Copyright © 2011 Timothy L. Bost

All rights reserved under all Copyright Conventions.

No part of this e-book may be reproduced, stored in a retrieval system, or transmitted by any means, electronic, mechanical, photocopying, recording, or otherwise for public or private use (other than for "fair use" as brief quotations embodied in articles and reviews), without written permission from the author.

While the publisher and author have used their best efforts in preparing this publication, they make no representation or warranties with respect to the accuracy or completeness of its contents, and specifically disclaim any implied warranties or merchantability or fitness for a particular purpose. No warrant may be created or extended by sales representatives or written sales materials. The advice and strategies contained herein may not be suitable for your situation, and you should consult a professional where appropriate. This publication is prepared from astrological information, news reports, cycle projections, and market observations which are believed to be accurate and reliable, but which cannot be guaranteed. Even with accurate information, past performance is no guarantee of future results. Speculation in securities and commodities involves considerable financial risk, and readers who plan to invest or speculate in any securities or commodities mentioned in this publication have the complete responsibility for making themselves fully aware of all the risks involved before they invest. The information presented in this publication should in no way be understood or construed as a solicitation or an offer to buy or sell any products or securities, nor should it be considered buy/sell advice. Neither the publisher nor author shall be liable for any loss of profit or other personal or commercial damages, including but not limited to special, incidental, consequential, or other damages.

Submit all requests for reprinting to:
Harmonic Research Associates
Post Office Box 1657
Sarasota, Florida 34230-1657 USA

Published in the United States of America by Harmonic Research Associates.

www.HarmonicResearchAssociates.com

ISBN-10: 1-933198-28-1
ISBN-13: 978-1-933198-28-6

EAN: 9781933198286

Table of Contents

Strategy, Systems and Success

During the past few decades I've had the opportunity to interact with a lot of traders in stocks, commodities, and options. Some of them have read my books or have been subscribers to my FinancialCyclesWeekly.com online. membership services; others have attended workshops and seminars that I have taught.

Still others have been clients seeking individual insight and assistance, either for help with business strategies, for specific insights that can move them into stronger alignment with their life purposes in their work, their relationships, and their educational and spiritual activities, or for transformative tools and processes that can make a big difference in the results that they are getting with their trading. Some of these traders have consulted with me for just one or two telephone sessions, which in their cases have been all they needed to turn their trading around. From time to time others have traveled to meet with me for extended tutoring and mentoring, spending two weeks or more in intensive daily sessions to create massive transformations in their ability to apply the astro-trading advantage to their market activity. While they have paid me between $15,000 and $20,000 for those coaching intensives, and have also incurred the cost of travel and lodging, it's invariably been a worthwhile investment for them.

Through these experiences, the tools and techniques for astro-trading have evolved to dramatically more effective levels. Thanks to that evolution it is now more feasible than ever before to understand the underlying rhythms and resonances of the markets, and to use that knowledge of vibrational harmonics to create ever-more accurate forecasts and ever-more profitable trading opportunities.

Traders no longer need to feel victimized by the vagaries of the markets, and they can once and for all abandon the erroneous belief that the markets are somehow against them, with unseen forces in the trading environment conspiring to create unfair losses.

While many markets are of course subject to manipulation, the wise trader can now choose simply to accept that fact while enjoying a broader (and much more profitable) perspective that rises above any active manipulation that may occur—the powerful and uniquely profitable advantage offered by more comprehensive cosmic viewpoints.

By adding this far-reaching perspective to the insights and analytical tools provided by market fundamentals and by technical analysis, today's independent-minded traders can begin to connect with the underlying Law of Vibration that drives all market activity, and thus can discover the astro-trading advantage for themselves.

As a result, it is now possible for trading to be a worthwhile part-time activity or a means of creating a solid supplemental income as well as a full-time pursuit reserved for professionals. In fact, the knowledgeable astro-trader can often out-perform even the most expert traders who choose to limit themselves to more conventional means of market analysis, money and trade management, and market timing.

The opportunities are indeed enormous, with the markets increasingly becoming steady streams of potential profit to an unprecedented degree. But along the way, one thing has become abundantly clear—unless today's traders actually learn to keep up with the evolving tools and techniques of astro-trading, they will miss out on a lot of the benefits that come with those approaches—and which also happen to be the benefits enjoyed through the eight Billionaire Strategies discussed in this book.

The gaps between ideas and action, and between superficial familiarity and in-depth knowledge, can be extraordinarily costly. If those gaps are present in your own market behavior you run a considerable risk of failure.

It was because of the growing potential for those critical gaps that this book came to be written. In these pages you will find landmarks and guideposts that can direct you toward greater trading profitability. But unless you take the concepts seriously and start applying them for yourself, you simply won't get the benefits the billionaires enjoy.

Measuring Wealth

What does it mean to be rich?

The response to that question is obviously a subjective matter. It depends on who you're asking, and on what they're thinking about when they reply.

What's rich for you many not be rich for me. What I consider rich today is probably going to be quite different from what was rich for me five years ago.

Being rich is also a relative consideration. It's sort of like being tall or being skinny—we can tell if we are rich if we compare ourselves to people who are poor, but does that make us super-rich, ultra-rich, or just plain affluent?

That kind of subjectivity and uncertainty is why it's useful to have objective standards of measurement, even if those standards are somewhat arbitrary. So we have the official "poverty line"—a specific dollar amount that defines the earnings threshold which determines eligibility for various sorts of public assistance.

On the flip side of poverty, we can also create specific levels of personal net worth or of annual earnings that represent a state of wealth.

Being a millionaire used to have that kind of status. From the early days of network television, with its dramatic program "The Millionaire", to the popular game show "Who Wants to Be a Millionaire" a few decades later, the idea of having $1,000,000 was promulgated in the popular consciousness as the ultimate standard of wealth.

But now, of course, being a millionaire is not at all what it used to be. It may still be a worthy goal in the developing world (take a look at the film "Slumdog Millionaire"), but with dollars buying less and less and with the growing numbers of newly-minted millionaires, it has lost a lot of its appeal, or at least its exclusivity.

That's why billionaire thinking is so important.

For the time being, anyway, having a personal net worth of at least $1 billion provides an unequivocal answer to the "what does it mean to be rich"question. While the ranks of billionaires are growing daily, the aggregate number of these individuals is still small enough that it represents a fairly exclusive club.

At the same time, however, reaching billionaire status is certainly not an insurmountable goal. We have all heard the tales of college students who create technological breakthroughs or come up with wildly popular marketing ideas and then become billionaires before the age of 30. Those tales aren't fiction.

Along the way, billionaire status has moved from being a vague symbol of incomprehensibly vast wealth to becoming a topic of daily discussion, not just in the pages of the Forbes lists of the world's most wealthy individuals, but also in debates about public policy, and casual cocktail party conversation, and in the flow of guests and gossip on television talk shows.

But billionaires are not just celebrities. Very few individuals are born into billionaire status, so being a billionaire represents a unique level of personal accomplishment, whether it's through entrepreneurship, deal-making, or investment and speculation.

It's precisely that focus on accomplishment that makes it worthwhile for us to pay attention to billionaire strategies in the stock market. While participation in the stock market is a widespread popular activity, with more than half of all Americans now owning stocks either individually or through mutual funds, the market perspectives of billionaires are especially valuable, both as sources of inspiration and as practical guidelines for enhanced performance.

When I mention billionaire attitudes and actions in the stock market, however, I'm not suggesting that all billionaires reach that level of affluence exclusively through participation in the stock market. Their wealth-generating actions and attitudes can be applied in virtually any field of endeavor, so they're worth taking a look at no matter what your field of activity may be.

But when billionaire strategies are implemented in the markets, they provide an enormous leverage and efficiency. And best of all, you don't have to be a billionaire to benefit from them!

A Personal Story

In the interest of full disclosure, I have a confession to make. At the time of this writing, in January 2011, I'm personally not a billionaire yet.

Although I'm certainly moving in that direction, I haven't yet reached that financial goal. While I remind myself regularly that I'm on my way, and while I'm constantly increasing my net worth, I do want to be honest with you and admit that I have not yet personally joined the ever-increasing ranks of the world's billionaires.

Even so, during my years of involvement with the financial markets, I've learned a lot about the billionaires of today and the billionaires of former generations. I've gained some remarkable insights into what makes them tick. I've learned a lot about who they are and where they come from, and more importantly I've learned how they became billionaires in the first place.

Along the way, I've discovered that many billionaires have certain characteristics in common. They do things that most other people simply aren't willing to do. They aren't afraid to take risks that most other people won't take, even if it makes them look a little bit foolish. And they have their own secret strategies for getting the kind of profitable knowledge, money-making information, and valuable insights that can increase their net worth day after day, week after week, and year after year.

One of the best things about billionaire strategies, the secrets that billionaires use to build and increase their fortunes and out of the markets, is that even though you and I may not personally be billionaires yet ourselves, we can get access to those secrets. We can crack the code of the billionaires' success. We can start right now to think like billionaires think, and do the things that billionaires do—and it won't cost us a billion dollars to do it!

By the way, that's one of the infallible principles of success in any field: if you want to be successful yourself, pick somebody who's already successful as your mentor, or at least pick them as a model for your own behavior. That same principle applies whether you want to improve your tennis game or your golf swing, whether you want to become a better parent or a better businessperson, or whether you want to uncover your full potential in reaching your personal goals.

If you really want to succeed, pick a top performer or a world-class expert as your mentor or your role model. Be willing to take some risks, to try new ideas, and to learn new ways of doing things, even if you feel a little bit foolish or uncomfortable when you first get started. When you start to get outstanding results, you'll discover that it's worth going through the potential uncertainty and embarrassment.

But whether or not you find it potentially embarrassing, f your goal is to increase your net worth and to enhance your financial well-being, then you need to model what you do on the actions and examples of financially successful people. Pay attention to the billionaire's secret, and follow billionaire strategies in every way that you can.

I'm probably like most people in that while I've sought new ways to increase my wealth and well-being, I've also been very concerned about how not to lose what I've already gained. That's why, as I've sought to learn the secrets of the billionaires, I've been especially pleased to discover that there are sound and proven strategies for protecting assets and investment capital, for keeping losses to a minimum, while at the same time grabbing opportunities for acquiring more financial leverage, for adding to the advantages that can make life more comfortable, more enjoyable, and more rewarding for you and the ones you love.

For me this process is a spiritual endeavor as well as a material one. Through my experiences in the markets and because of my exposure to important billionaire strategies, I've had countless opportunities to explore new dimensions of my personal faith and to open up to a richer understanding of my full potential in alignment with divine plan and purpose. My feeling is that when you can do things that simultaneously improve your relationships, strengthen your faith, expand your financial potential, and optimize your physical and mental well-being, you're getting outcomes that are worth a reasonable amount of risk.

Having that key understanding has helped me feel safer in taking exactly those kinds of risks, the ones that are most likely to get significant results. It has also helped me give myself permission to explore areas that opened up new horizons in my life. My choices in some instances may seem strange to some other people, as I have followed unlikely paths that have brought me some amazing rewards.

One of those areas is astrology. It's a rich and fascinating field, and it has offered me lots of extremely useful insights for quite some time. In fact, I've now had over 40 years of experience in astrology, and for the last 23 years, as I've been working to understand the hidden secrets of billionaires, I've been specializing in financial astrology, with an intense focus on the kinds of astro-trading tools that create breakthrough success in the markets.

In 1988, when I was just starting to get profitable results from my research in this field, I began publication of the *Financial Cycles* newsletter, which began as a monthly publication. It's now a weekly membership subscription publication, *FinancialCyclesWeekly.com*, which is sent out via e-mail to readers around the world each week and includes access to a special members-only website for astro-traders.

If visited that website if you've seen my market commentaries quoted in **Barron's** magazine, **Bridge News**, and other financial publications, or if you've seen me interviewed on the "Commodity Classics" TV program, you'll recognize the fact that financial astrology has become increasingly accepted as a important tool in the investment community and in the speculative world of stock and commodity trading.

While I certainly appreciate the personal acknowledgment and am glad to see astro-trading and financial astrology moving into the mainstream, the truth of the matter is that my gaining recognition as an expert in the field of financial astrology was far from an automatic process. The challenge was more than just one of having to deal with ignorant prejudices and preconceptions about astrology. I certainly had to deal with those misconceptions, of course, but there were many other obstacles that I was obliged to contend with as well, including the necessity of having to work under some fairly inhibiting material circumstances.

When I first got involved in this area, I was a dedicated student of astrology but I had no money to invest. In fact, I was living in a ramshackle house that was a mile down a dirt road in the rural hills of western North Carolina. We had electricity in the house but no running water, and in those lean days I was feeding my family with vegetables grown in the back yard, along with a little help from food stamps from time to time.

As I began my research into the connections between market trends and astrological phenomena, I made regular trips to the public library, where I would copy down stock and commodity prices from the Wall Street Journal, putting the figures in a spiral notebook. Then I'd take my notebook home and chart out the prices on big sheets of graph paper, trying to figure out what was going on in the heavens and how the market action had been reflecting the celestial events.

This was in the day before personal computers were available, so the work was very slow and challenging. But it gave me a good foundation, and I began to develop a solid understanding of what makes financial astrology work, and why it is one of the most closely-guarded secrets of the billionaires. Today, of course, with computers available and easy internet access to market data, it's much, much easier to get started in financial astrology, and nothing stands in the way of your profiting from this knowledge yourself—as a student of market astrology, as an analyst with an extra edge, or as an astro-trader on either a part-time or a full-time basis.

This is very powerful knowledge. During the last few decades, I have learned a lot about how astrology functions in the markets, and about how it can be used to increase the profitability of trading and investing, and to transform your relationship with money. It's very practical, and it's very profitable, too!

That's the experience, and the tremendous change in my own life, that has brought me to where I am today. And because of the many incredible rewards of that experience and that tremendous change, because of the success of that journey from dirt roads and the public library to a clear understanding of the cosmic resonances that move the markets, I'm especially eager to share this knowledge with you. After all, if learning about astro-trading brings you any positive results at all, or even if it improves the profitability of your investments by just one or two percentage points, it can ultimately create a massive transformation in your life as well.

The eight billionaire strategies for breakthrough stock market success are also eight compelling reasons why you should personally consider adding financial astrology to your trading and investment toolkit. I think you'll find that these reasons, and the ideas behind them, will give you more than enough motivation to explore this amazing moneymaking tool for yourself. At least I hope so, because it can mark the beginning of an exciting new phase in your personal financial well-being.

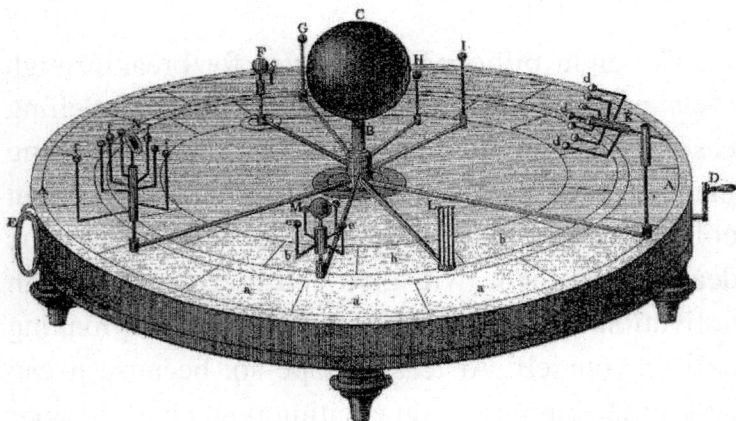

Planetary Cycles and the Markets

But before we get started in exploring those eight billionaire strategies and the corresponding reasons for considering financial astrology as a part of your own program in trading and investing, it's probably a good idea to say a couple of things about astrology itself. And here I speak from personal experience.

You know, I get some extremely interesting reactions when I meet people for the first time and tell them what I do for a living. It's the kind of thing that happens at a business gathering or a social event and it's so tangled up in confusion that I'm sometimes tempted to make up something ordinary-sounding just so I can avoid the conversational challenges.

But when I say I am a financial astrologer, the most typical reaction I get is just a blank stare or a puzzled look. I usually hasten to explain that being a financial astrologer means that I examine planetary cycles, and then I apply them to the changing trends in the stock market.

That attempt at an explanation on my part usually changes the reaction I'm getting a little bit. But in most cases, the response is one of outright disbelief or sometimes even laughter, especially if the person I'm talking to feels that he or she is already very knowledgeable in the workings of the markets. Sometimes the response will be more of a knowing smile instead of an obvious chuckle, but the message is clear just the same—using astrology in the world of finance is obviously something that should not be taken seriously.

I honestly can't say that I really blame them when they laugh. After all, most people have some real misconceptions, and often very strange ones, about what astrology actually is.

They usually base their understanding of it on their experiences in reading the horoscope columns on popular websites or in the newspaper. Those newspaper horoscope columns can be wonderfully entertaining, and they are in fact based on some real astrological factors. They're typically grounded in a few of the most significant things that professional astrologers look at when they make their forecasts. But the stuff that goes into the newspaper horoscope column is just a tiny fraction of the complex understanding of planetary dynamics that makes real astrology work.

The application of astrology to the financial markets is a different matter altogether. It has practically nothing to do with what you will read in the daily newspaper horoscope. It's not about what zodiac sign you are, who you are the most compatible with, or whether this is a good day or a bad day for you.

Financial astrology involves a whole lot more than just the analysis of Sun signs. It has a long and honorable history, and it has a proven track record of success. Because that's the case, it deserves serious attention from anyone who wants to reach big financial goals more quickly and effortlessly. That's especially true if your aspiration is to become a billionaire

In ancient times astrology was used in India and in Assyria to forecast economic trends and to improve the profitability of business transactions. It was about 27 hundred years ago that Thales of Miletus made his fortune by using his knowledge of astrology to corner the market for olive oil. And in more modern times, J. P. Morgan, America's first billionaire, regularly sought the advice of the famous astrologer Evangeline Adams, who kept him informed of the planetary cycles that could be expected to be reflected in business trends.

In fact, it was Evangeline Adams who remarked that "J. Pierpont Morgan, the world's biggest financier, drove the world before him because he had astrology behind him." And it was J. P. Morgan's use of astrology that first led me to suspect that financial astrology was perhaps one of the most valuable secrets of the billionaires, if not the biggest billionaire's secret of them all!

By the early years of the 20th century, some of the most successful people on Wall Street were using astrology to improve their financial fortunes.

George Bayer used astrological analysis to trade in wheat and in the stock market. W. D. Gann, the legendary genius who developed his own system of technical analysis for forecasting trends in the stock and commodity markets, also used astrology, and he became one of the most successful speculators of his day.

In fact, during his 50-year career in the markets, Gann reputedly earned more than many other traders. His reputation was legendary. In fact, it is said that W. D. Gann earned over $50 million in the stock and commodity markets before his death in 1955, and his market forecasts proved to be accurate more than 85% of the time. While Gann was certainly an astute trader, he also had a dramatic advantage in the markets, because he knew how to put astrology to work.

Discovering Real Wealth

During the past 23 years, I have studied and applied financial astrology in my own work, using it in my own research, in my forecasting, and in my active trading in stocks and in equities options. The benefits have been enormous. Financial astrology has literally opened up new worlds for me, and I'm constantly excited about the new horizons that keep opening up in this fascinating field.

My aim in this little book is to share some of that enthusiasm with you, and also to give back a little bit of what I've gained so that you can share in the treasures of astro-trading and in the fantastic money-making potential that financial astrology offers.

I've said that in discussing eight billionaire strategies for breakthrough stock market success, I also plan to share some compelling reasons with you today for getting involved with astrology in the markets. But this is far from a comprehensive or exhaustive list.

There are actually a whole lot more benefits that you can gain from financial astrology than the ones I'm about to mention in these pages. And when you improve your financial situation, it's possible for many other aspects of your life to fall into place as well, including your health, your family life, and the richness of your intellectual and spiritual growth. When you experience abundance in all these areas, you can't help but discover what real wealth is all about.

Even so, I wanted to give you this short list here, just to fire up your imagination a little bit, and to get you started thinking about the possibilities that await you if you do decide to move ahead in your personal exploration of this amazing way of improving your net worth.

Eight Billionaire Strategies

1. Identify big opportunities before they occur.

2. Improve the timing of short-term speculation.

3. Take risks that are in sync with long-term cycles.

4. Know your own unique strengths and weaknesses.

5. Embrace change as a natural part of your financial progress.

6. Refine your forecasting skills to identify profitable opportunities at low risk.

7. Keep yourself open to new information, to fresh insights and ideas, and to first-time experiences.

8. Accumulate and preserve capital through effective money management.

Billionaire Strategy #1:
Identify Big Opportunities
Before They Occur

There's perhaps nothing more valuable in or out of the markets as the ability to anticipate opportunities ahead of time. In many cases this seemingly uncanny ability is really nothing more than common sense—spotting resources that are currently undervalued, for example, with some level of assurance that they will be worth a great deal more at some future date.

In many cases that kind of common-sense observation can be combined with advance knowledge of specific circumstances that are likely to impact supply-and-demand dynamics, such as the assumption that the onset of extremely hot weather will create an increased interest in fans and air conditioners.

When this kind of awareness is brought to bear in situations that specifically relate to the markets, it can help us spot long-term trends and cycles more effectively. When it is combined with the tools of technical analysis, it will send us for a look at weekly and monthly price charts, giving us the advantage of longer-term perspectives.

It's also worth noting that this all-important strategy of identifying big opportunities before they occur gets considerable support from the unique insights that are provided through the knowledge and application of financial astrology. In fact, one of the most valuable characteristics of astrology is that it gives us the ability to identify big opportunities far enough in advance that we can plan for them ahead of time and profit accordingly.

Financial astrology gives us a window on the future. With the right knowledge and understanding of this amazing discipline, we can tell far ahead of time when major trends are about to change.

With that kind of advance knowledge, with the unique early warning system that financial astrology provides, we can protect ourselves from the adverse effects of financial crisis. Even more importantly, we can develop strategies for improving our profits and enhancing our net worth, whether the markets are going up, or the markets are going down.

That's not only valuable information in terms of dollars and cents. It's also incredibly valuable in the kind of peace of mind and sense of security that we can add to our personal and financial planning. With the ability to see big opportunities—and big challenges—ahead of time, we have a much higher likelihood of staying "healthy, wealthy, and wise."

Billionaire Strategy #2: Improve the Timing of Short-Term Speculation

While it's important to prepare for long-range opportunities before they unfold, there are also times when opportunities pop up more unexpectedly. When that happens, we typically have a fairly narrow window within which we can take action that might prove profitable.

That's an especially significant guideline if we're trading actively in any market arena. While the most certain notion about market behavior is simply that it will fluctuate, if you have an understanding of the ups and downs of that fluctuation, you can radically increase the overall profitability of your trading.

This is another key area in which financial astrology and the specific skills of astro-trading can play a vital role. It's something that should interest you a great deal if you are already actively trading in the markets, or if you have ever dreamed about making your living as an active trader. Financial astrology is an extraordinarily powerful tool for enhancing the timing of short-term trades.

At this point it's probably wise for me to issue a warning, even if you've heard it before. Short-term trading is not for everyone, and it may not be right for you.

In the first place, short-term trading takes some working capital. It also takes a lot of mental and emotional discipline, and it can certainly involve considerable financial risk.

But if you have already made up your mind about short-term trading, if you are currently a short-term trader in the markets, or if you aspire to become one, then you will definitely want to learn about the ways that financial astrology can enhance your trading performance. I'm confident that once you gain the astro-trading advantage, you'll never look back toward the old ways you used to behave in the markets.

In a nutshell, financial astrology and the insights it provides into planetary dynamics and their impact on market trends can provide us with important tools for refining our trading strategies. Astrology can help us identify better entry points and exit points for the trades that we take. It can also help us determine the times when we may not want to be actively trading at all.

The bottom line here is that if you're an active trader, financial astrology can help you bring home bigger trading profits. Gaining the astro-trading advantage is worth the time and energy you must spend to master it.

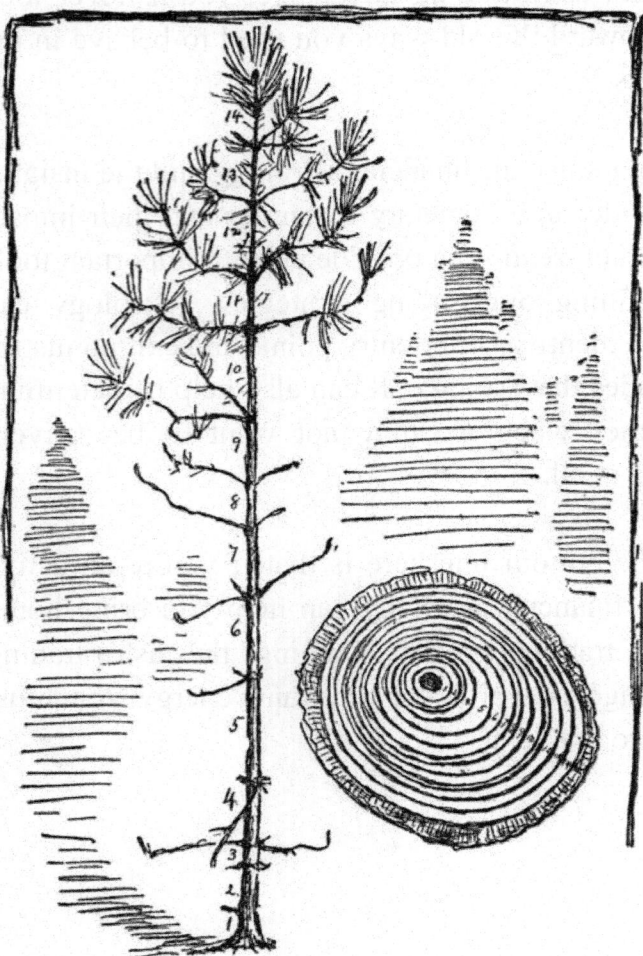

Billionaire Strategy #3: Take Risks That Are in Sync with Long-Term Cycles

We live in a turbo-charged, high-intensity, high-speed world. The constant flow of information, the always-on, always-connected nature of relationships, and the perpetual demands of multi-tasking give us enormous power and leverage, but they create enormous stress as well. And it's exactly that point of dichotomy that helps define billionaire thinking.

If you are always feeling overwhelmed, if you're perpetually finding yourself becoming a victim in the various situations life hands you, you're unlikely to acquire the insights, attitudes, and habits that create billionaire status.

The billionaires, on the other hand, are typically much more able to embrace the chaos, to step back from the tension and the confusion, and to discover opportunities that other people miss. That big-picture thinking gives them a unique advantage.

Big-picture thinking is useful in entrepreneurial enterprises as well, and it's essential any effective negotiating and deal-making. But it's also extraordinarily valuable if you're participating in the markets.

How many potentially devastating trading mistakes can be avoided simply by altering the time frame of the charts and projections we are examining? If you are caught up in the fluctuations of tick data or of one-minute price bars, it's easy to be surprised by the trend information revealed in weekly or monthly charts.

Even more importantly, an awareness of broader time frames can help us identify significant underlying trends and cycles more easily. When we synchronize our speculative efforts with longer-term cycles, we can make dramatic shifts in the ratio of the rewards we get to the risks that we take.

That's another area where financial astrology comes into play. It offers you a better understanding of long-term cycles as well as short-term phenomena. Although financial astrology serves us well in revealing the short-term dynamics in the markets, it's also about slower, bigger changes that have much more long-lasting effects.

If you are personally more of a long-term investor, rather than an active trader, you'll certainly want to gain the knowledge that financial astrology offers you in developing sensible investment plans to take full advantage of the ups and downs in the business cycle and of the ebb and flow of the world economy.

There's an interesting thing about studying cycles. Most of us have had some personal experience with shifting trends in the economy, and with the impact of cycles on our job situations, on our livelihood, and on our ability to make ends meet. In some cases, we have experienced personal windfalls as a result of changing times, and in other cases we have perhaps been less fortunate, and we have suffered unduly in catastrophic situations because we weren't really prepared to weather a sudden change in the prevailing economic trends.

I certainly hope that you've had more windfalls than catastrophes in your life, but if you're like most of us you've experienced at least some of both. That variety of experience is enough to give you some knowledge of the validity of cycles at a gut level—we all go through ups and downs, and the pattern seems to repeat itself.

But the big question is, exactly WHEN will that pattern repeat? Here's a key bit of information: while cycles create those alternate ups and downs, not all cycles are regular rhythms. In other words, the ups and downs aren't always evenly spaced out. They don't always take place at consistent intervals, like clockwork. This is something that billionaires keep in their consciousness.

Not all cycles are rhythms. The repetitions will be there, but they don't always take place when we expect them to. In many cases, the true nature of cycles seems to be quite mysterious.

Perhaps more than any other tool at our disposal, an understanding of astrology can unlock the truth about cycles. Astrology, and especially the astrology of the markets, can help reveal the hidden dimensions of cycles, the factors and nuances that escape the attention of casual observers. With knowledge of planetary dynamics and their complex interactions, we can profit from an in-depth understanding of the ways that cycles can impact our lives, as well as get some insights into when those impacts will actually occur. That kind of knowledge is what empowers billionaires to take risks that harmonize with long-term cycles.

Of course even with advanced knowledge, we can still mess things up. As human beings we have a seemingly infinite capacity for making mistakes, for doing things in exactly the wrong way, even when we should know better. And that's why the fourth billionaire strategy is so important.

Billionaire Strategy #4:
Know Your Own Unique
Strengths and Weaknesses

Most billionaires have a unique capacity for understanding themselves, as well as the unique ability to turn realistic self-assessment into extraordinary personal profits. The great message of the ancient Greek philosopher Socrates was to "know thyself," and that kind of genuine self-knowledge is one of the characteristics that billionaires share. It's a message that they take to heart, and with real self-knowledge they automatically gain an ability to set priorities more effectively, to make decisions that enable them to delegate key tasks in critical situations, and to capitalize more fully on their unique personal talents, skills, and strengths.

While billionaires are likely to embrace a variety of tools and methodologies for enhancing their self-knowledge, there are few approaches that can equal the compelling insights provided by astrology. Astrology can not only provide us with a better understanding of ourselves—it can open the gateway to richer, more profitable possibilities as we explore more fulfilling ways of expressing our natural capabilities. It's when billionaires open up to that kind of intensified self-expression that they are often most likely to engage in the kind of idea-generating and action-taking that create even more massive wealth.

It was C. G. Jung, the world-renowned psychologist, who said that "Astrology represents the summation of the psychological knowledge of antiquity." In other words, if we want to understand what really makes us tick, we can gain invaluable help from a knowledge of astrology, and if we put that knowledge to practical use the benefits are truly astonishing.

The fact is, you are a unique individual, unlike any other person on the planet. And that's what real astrology reveals, as opposed to the pop astrology that you'll find in the newspaper horoscope columns or on the websites that feature lucky numbers and psychic 900 lines.

Real astrology is not about locking you into one of twelve limited pigeonholes, based on the month you were born in. It's about understanding what makes you different and unique, what gives you strength and where your potential weaknesses are. It's about knowing how you can use your unique capabilities to make the best possible decisions for your life, and then act on those decisions.

Real astrology provides practical, personalized information that's uniquely about you, and it's there to help you reach your full potential in taking advantage of all the opportunities that life gives you.

This is especially true if we are involved in the markets. In order to be successful as traders or as investors, we need to consider the three components of the all-important Trading Triad.

First of all, we have the overall market itself and the prevailing market conditions that can impact our ability to trade profitably. Is the market in a rally, or is it in a bearish trend? We need to have at least some understanding of these factors in order to be successful, and the Market Knowledge part of the Trading Triad gives us that kind of information.

The next consideration is the trade itself. Exactly what are we trading, and how big is our position going to be? What are the specific conditions that lead us to believe we can be successful by entering a trade at this particular time? Making money in the markets depends on being in the right trade at the right time, with the right kind of money management at work protecting us behind the scenes. With the Trading Skill portion of the Trading Triad we have an opportunity to take the kind of actions that can enhance our outcomes in the markets.

The third part of the Trading Triad is the trader. That's the part of the trade that is ultimately the most vulnerable, and it's the portion of the Trading Triad that is unfortunately the most often overlooked. Even if we have clear-cut rules for making money in the markets, if we personally don't always follow those rules, we can't be successful. And astrology offers us a unique tool for gaining insights into ourselves and into the kind of behavior that can make or break us in the markets.

The more thoroughly we understand ourselves and our built-in mechanisms for self-sabotage, for shooting ourselves in the foot, the more likely we are to avoid destructive behavior and then to walk away with profits at the end of the trading day. So in the light of this critically important Billionaire Strategy, financial astrology is personally valuable for us as traders and investors as well.

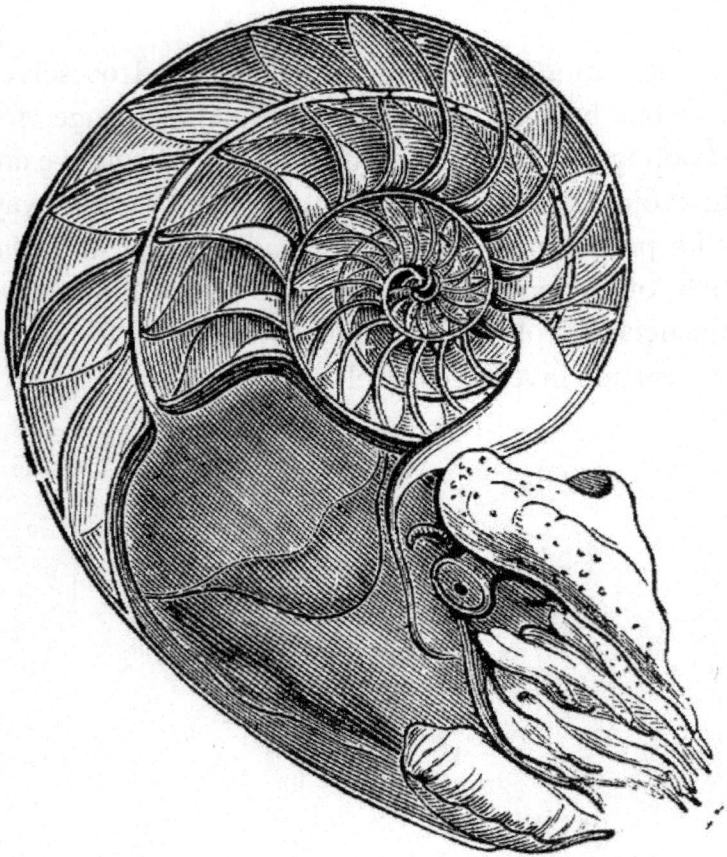

Billionaire Strategy #5: Embrace Change as a Natural Part of Your Financial Progress

Change can be a very threatening thing for an individual who is locked into poverty consciousness. But for someone with a millionaire mindset, change is something to be welcomed. It is, after all, one of the universal laws that empower growth in nature, the progression of the seasons, the fullest expressions of human capabilities, and the evolution of the planet as a whole. It is what enables small businesses to become big businesses, students to gain increasing skill and move toward mastery, and bright ideas to be made manifest in material reality.

In the markets, of course, change is the place where the potential for profits resides. If we buy a stock today, and then sell it a year from now, we can reap the rewards if the change in price has been in a positive direction. But without any change in price occurring, our speculative efforts will have been a total waste. Not only will we fail to make any money on the transaction; we will also have lost potentially profitable opportunities by keeping our capital frozen in a nonproductive market position. Without change, we can watch our market opportunities vanish before our eyes. When there's enough change going on in the markets, there is virtually no limit to the rewards that we can capture.

A natural process of change is also out and lay and beautifully expressed in the movements of the heavenly bodies, from the progression of the phases of the Moon to the intricate interrelationships of the outer planets. That's why financial astrology and the tools of astro-trading offer us yet another reward— they give us a way of aligning ourselves with the natural flow of things.

That notion of aligning with the flow may sound a little vague or actually a little bit mystical, but it's actually an extremely important consideration if we are going to be successful financially. If we are connected in harmonizing ways with the natural flow, we can be much more successful in our market endeavors. But if our efforts go against the natural grain, we are likely to find it much more difficult, if not altogether impossible, to earn significant financial returns through our trading activities.

One of the key characteristics of truly successful people is that they embrace change instead of being frightened by it. That's true for the world's billionaires, and it can be true for you, too!

A genuinely wealthy mindset, a real prosperity consciousness, is characterized by an understanding that change is good. No matter how uncomfortable it may seem at the time, change always offers us an opportunity to learn the new things that we need to know. When we assimilate this greater knowledge, we can accomplish greater things, and accumulate greater wealth.

Real astrology helps us understand that change is not only inevitable; it is also completely natural. And when we act in accordance with that natural flow, we can become successful much more effortlessly.

In some respects, this is actually just common sense. For example, if we have a passion for snow skiing, we may want to pursue that sport at every available opportunity. But if we plan a skiing trip in the middle of the summer when it's 95° Fahrenheit outside, then we are likely to be disappointed if we pack up our skis or strap on our ice skates. So we have a choice. We can either cancel our plans for skiing at that particular time, or we can find a different location, one with much colder temperatures and maybe even some man-made snow, in order to pursue our recreational passion.

Likewise, we might have plans for a picnic. We may have even packed a big basket of fruit and cheese, and picked out a particularly delicious bottle of wine to share with a special someone on this occasion. However, if the weather forecaster lets us know that there's a 90% chance of rain that day, we are once again faced with the need to make some choices. Are we going to cancel our plans for the outing, or are we going to go ahead with the picnic anyway, and just take along an umbrella?

While I know these examples of dealing with the weather may seem overly simplistic, they illustrate the importance of working in accordance with the natural flow of things. Financial astrology helps us understand the natural flow of things in the markets as well, revealing patterns that are not always as obvious as the changes in the weather. When we understand what those patterns are, and when we act in accordance with them, our financial future is far more secure. And with that added sense of security, we are far more likely to take the kinds of well-considered risks in the markets that can bring us significant rewards.

Billionaire Strategy #6: Refine Your Forecasting Skills to Identify Profitable Opportunities at Low Risk

One of the most inspiring things about billionaires is that they are almost universally committed to lifelong learning. That learning may not take place within the framework of an organized educational structure—in fact, there are many billionaires who don't have college degrees. But whether the learning comes through classrooms, comic books, or hard-knocks experience in the world of commerce, what's characteristic of the billionaire mindset is a dedication to acquiring more knowledge and to applying it in strategic ways.

That kind of strategic thinking provides obvious advantages in just about any kind of endeavor, whether it's organizing a new business, inventing a new concept or product, or uncovering innovative new ways of presenting effective marketing messages. And it goes without saying that strategic thinking and creative foresight and make a huge difference in the results we can get when we put our money at risk in the markets.

Once again, financial astrology has an important role to play in advancing this Billionaire Strategy. As the tools and techniques of modern astro-trading continue to evolve, this growing discipline brings us an increasing variety of ways in which we can improve the quality of our market forecasting.

That's not a small benefit. There are, of course, plenty of market pundits and commentators around, and plenty of market forecasts available. In fact, it's just about impossible to avoid hearing market forecasts, and when everything is said and done, very few of them actually turn out to be worth too much. At least that's been my experience, no matter who is doing the forecasting.

But financial astrology gives us an extra set of tools to apply to market forecasting. Typical market analysis and forecasting involves either the fundamental approach or the technical approach, or some kind of combination of the two.

The fundamental approach to market analysis is all about what's happening in the physical world. If we're analyzing a company, for example, we will look at the financial statements to see whether or not the company is making any money. We will study its management team, we'll take a look at production and distribution costs, examine its marketing strategies, explore its competitive environment, and so forth. Then, based on our analysis of these fundamental factors in the operations of the company, we will come up with a comprehensive assessment of what the company is actually worth, and what its potential is for future growth and profitability. We will look at earnings trends, revenue projections, and the data from mergers and acquisitions. And we will base our forecasts for that company's stock on that fundamental analysis.

In contrast to the fundamental approach, there are some analysts and market forecasters who prefer technical analysis, which means that they look at the historical performance of the stock itself rather than studying the day-to-day details of the company's operations. Technical analysts like to use charts of stock prices, and their basic idea is that all of the most relevant information about a company and its financial prospects is encapsulated in the price action for the stock, and in the changes of trend expressed by the stock price over a period of time.

In its most refined form, tackle analysis gives us tools for pattern recognition that help us to see new opportunities in emerging because of their similarity to market configurations from the past. Even more advanced market technicians use the Fibonacci ratios, patterns of vibrational resonance that clearly connect market movements to the universal rhythms that manifest throughout the natural world.

But financial astrology gives us a third approach, a third tool to use in market analysis and market forecasting. Along with the traditional approaches of fundamental analysis and technical analysis, we can also use planetary analysis, or financial astrology.

When we do that, we get a non-correlated confirming factor to use in our market forecasting, and with the introduction of that additional factor, we can get more accurate, more robust, and more useful forecasts. This sixth Billionaire Strategy for enhanced performance in the markets thus gains a great deal from financial astrology, which can help us in producing more accurate and more profitable forecasts.

Billionaire Strategy #7:
Keep Yourself Open to New Information, to Fresh Insights and Ideas, and to First-Time Experiences

Billionaires have the essential knowledge that in the markets, as in life in general, there's no intrinsically good or bad situation—there's only opportunity.

Staying open to opportunity is about staying open to new ideas and innovations. The billionaire mindset is one which is always reach to stretch, to imagine new possibilities, and to dream bigger dreams, no matter what inspires them.

Bill Gates acknowledged this mindset when he said that "I really had a lot of dreams when I was a kid, and I think a great deal of that grew out of the fact that I had a chance to read a lot." That's the kind of thinking that's typical of the highest levels of prosperity consciousness.

Being open-minded is an activity, not a static state. Unless we are actively seeking new experiences we are unlikely to connect with the opportunities that can ultimately make the biggest differences in our lives. But if we regularly visit new places, get to know new people, read unfamiliar magazines, try different kinds of foreign foods, and actively consider ideas and arguments that take us out of our intellectual comfort zones, we are far more likely to ready and receptive when opportunities unexpectedly present themselves.

That's especially true in the markets. In order to trade effectively, we need to craft a comprehensive trading plan and then stick with that plan consistently. But the profits in trading come to us when, within the context and structure of our trading plan, we are able to spot extraordinary opportunities and take advantage of them. In a sense it's very much like playing tennis—the net and the baselines define the court and restrict the playing area, but within that context we can place a smashing serve, return a volley, challenge our opponent, and find all sorts of opportunities for creative play.

In the markets, our trading plan acts like the net on the tennis court, defining the rules and developmental processes that will keep us on target toward our goals. But we are constantly on the lookout for fresh insights, for the bits of information that can help us determine prevailing market trends and position ourselves accordingly.

But no matter what we are doing to broaden our horizons and to keep our mind open and ready to receive new perspectives, the process can be considerably enhanced when we add astrology to the mix. Financial astrology can spontaneously open our minds to fresh experiences, to new and surprising connections in the world around us.

That independent urge toward creative new explorations may seem like an odd kind of benefit to gain from deciding to use a powerful new financial tool. But whether it seems odd or not, it's a benefit that's very concrete, and extremely useful as well. Any billionaire will tell you that.

When we approach life with an open mind, we can expand our creativity enormously. We can open ourselves up to a richer, more fulfilling awareness of who we really are, so that we can connect with our full potential in more expressive and more satisfying ways. That kind of awareness can be tremendously rewarding in every area of our lives—in our work, in our recreation, in our personal development, and in our relationships.

The kind of awareness that astrological thinking can wake up inside of us combines an openness to fresh possibilities, an intimate knowledge of our own personal potential, and a built-in ability to think outside of the box.

And while there can be considerable personal payoffs from that sort of enriched awareness, the financial payoffs can be enormous, too. We naturally become more alert to new opportunities. We learn to look at potential risks and potential rewards from a more energized and a more enlightened perspective. We can spot emerging trends more rapidly, and come up with ways to profit from those trends more effortlessly and more spontaneously. That can mean much greater profits from our trading, so this opening up of our mental floodgates is certainly not something that we should take lightly. It's a genuine benefit.

Billionaire Strategy #8: Accumulate and Preserve Capital through Effective Money Management

Billionaire Warren Buffett has two cardinal rules which provide a key to the final Billionaire Strategy we are discussing here, the commitment to accumulating and preserving capital through effective money management.

Despite his personal brilliance at values-based long-term investing, and despite the fact that his enormous wealth and business acumen have earned him international celebrity status, Buffett is not a man to waste words, and that was certainly the case when he was asked about how to achieve financial success.

As Buffett so succinctly put it: "Rule No. 1: Never lose money. Rule No. 2: Never forget Rule No. 1".

While that may have been Buffett's idea of a witty aphorism, it's nevertheless a key concept for anchoring billionaire consciousness, and it's an absolutely essential bit of advice for traders, whether or not they are billionaires.

As such, it underscores yet another core advantage of financial astrology and astro-trading. Even though it is probably the simplest and the most obvious consideration of all, we want to be sure we don't overlook it.

If you want to model your actions on billionaire behavior, you will want to consider adding financial astrology to your investment and trading toolkit simply because it can help you make much more money.

Like any other financial tool, astrology does have its limits. If you don't use it correctly, you won't get the best possible results. You have to take the ideas it offers and turn them into actions. But using astrology in the markets gives you such strong advantages, and enhances your ability to anticipate and deal with change so dramatically, that the change in your money-making potential can honestly be quite amazing.

This key notion—the ability to make money more effectively—is so compelling that I really don't think I need to go into too much more detail about it. Ultimately, of course its importance depends a lot on you. You may choose to become an astro-trader or not depending on your goals and your personal circumstances. But if you really want to become a billionaire, you simply can't afford to ignore the astro-trading advantage.

Of course becoming a billionaire may not be your personal aim. But no matter what your financial goals are, if making more money in the markets is a high priority for you, and if you want to have an easier time making that money, then financial astrology is definitely something you will want to consider taking a look at. Apply whatever parts you choose to your own individual situation and then get prepared to reap the benefits.

Strategies and Action Steps

At the end of the day, you're likely to discover that the most powerful and efficient way of cultivating billionaire attitudes for yourself is by exploring astrology and astro-trading. Each of the major reasons you should be finding out more about financial astrology. Also coincide with one of the Billionaire Strategies.

First of all, using astrology will help you identify big opportunities ahead of time so that you can take full advantage of them. When you can identify opportunities before they actually occur, you are well on your way to gaining one of the biggest advantages enjoyed by billionaires.

You can also activate the second Billionaire Strategy by using astro-trading techniques to improve the timing for your short-term trading.

Astrology gives you a much better understanding of long-term cycles. That's the kind of insight that will help you take appropriate risks at the best possible times, in keeping with billionaire strategy #3.

Astrology is also aligned with the advice of Socrates. It will help you understand yourself more completely, both as a person and as a trader. And when you know your own unique strengths and weaknesses, you can avoid crippling market mistakes.

By helping you align your risk-taking activities with the natural flow of cosmic processes, astrology can make it much easier for you to move effortlessly in and out of the markets. You will be able to welcome change in a way that moves you steadily toward your long-term financial goals.

Once you master the tools and techniques of effective astro-trading, it will improve the quality of your market analysis and your market forecasting. Through this refinement of your forecasting skills you will become increasingly able to identify profitable opportunities at low risk.

It takes an open mind to consider adding the astro-trading advantage to your personal engagement in the markets. That is especially true if you have misconceptions about the true nature of astrology, or if you have never personally encountered the astonishing clarity that financial astrology can bring to your understanding of the markets.

But once you open your mind to astrology, it in turn will open your mind even more, exposing you to new and surprising possibilities, possibilities for enhancing your wealth and for expanding your own personal potential. As you learn to keep yourself open to new information, to fresh insights and ideas, and to first-time experiences, you will be assimilating some of the core values that can make billionaire thinking and the billionaire lifestyle a reality.

And finally, of course, you will want to explore financial astrology and astro-trading because they can help you make more money.

I hope all that sounds good to you, whether or not you have personal plans to become a billionaire. But if it does, you're going to be faced with an important question: how will you personally go about exploring financial astrology? How will you put it to work for you?

There are several possible answers to that question. The answer that is right for you depends a lot on the kind of time and resources you are willing to dedicate to the financial astrology process and to mastering the skills of astro-trading. It also depends on the kind of person that you are.

Are you an individual who can't wait to roll up your sleeves and get involved in some serious study? Are you eager to reach new levels of understanding as your gain personal experience through lots of trial and error? Or do you prefer to let someone else do most of the work for you, so that you can just check in from time to time and take advantage of information and insights which can enhance your income and add to the profitability of your trading?

Your first alternative is to become a financial astrologer yourself. This is an immensely rewarding endeavor, but it takes a lot of work. It includes both some serious study requirements and the need for lots of disciplined practice. This path involves plenty of trial and error along the way as you master the nuances of this very complex, and very powerful, set of tools. It's a path that has a tremendous payoff, but it definitely involves a serious ongoing commitment on your part, if your aim is to become a financial astrologer yourself.

If this is the right path for you, you will almost certainly want to find a coach or mentor to guide you along the path towards astro-trading mastery. When you have the ongoing advice and support of someone who has had more experience in astro-trading than you have, you can give yourself an incredible boost, and save a lot of the time that might otherwise go into a long and laborious learning process. The best strategy is to find an expert mentor; if you connect with the right person the learning experience will ultimately prove to be worth many times more than the tuition price you pay.

But of course, not everyone is cut out to be a financial astrologer, and not everyone is willing to invest the years of study and practice that it takes to get a basic level of competence in this field.

If the path of becoming an astrologer yourself is not for you, there are other alternatives available. If you have an interest in astro-trading and financial astrology and what they can do for you, you certainly shouldn't abandon the idea of using them to improve the results you are getting from the market.

In fact, you might want to pursue the second alternative. You might wish to learn just enough about financial astrology so that you can improve your performance in the markets without making a serious commitment to long-term extended study or to rigorous daily practice.

Take your time to explore the basics of using astrology in the stock market. Do some reading, listen to financial astrology lectures, and review workshop DVDs. Take a look at the way astrology functions in the markets, and see for yourself what works and what doesn't work, and get clear about what makes the most sense to you. Then decide for yourself how much you will use it, and in what ways you will add it to your personal trading and investment plan. Once you have made up your mind about how much you want to apply it in your own trading program, then you can go about getting additional instruction and perhaps a little bit of coaching as well, so that you can stay focused on the task of acquiring a very specific set of profit-making tools. In fact, some coaching or mentoring services can be especially appropriate for this level of involvement with financial astrology and astro-trading, since a good coach can help you determine ahead of time just what kind of tools and experiences will be the most helpful to you as you devise your own individualized trading plan and then put it to the test with real money in the markets.

Finally, you may personally prefer to get the money-making insights that financial astrology has to offer and put them to work in your own trading and investing, all without learning very much about the how or the why financial astrology works.

There's absolutely nothing wrong with that approach. After all, you don't have to know how to change a spark plug in your car in order to be able to drive your car to the grocery store. So why should you have to know what astrology really is and how it actually works to be able to enjoy its money-making benefits?

The fact is, you don't. With the kinds of resources that are available today, you can get access to the latest thinking from the world's finest financial astrologers, and then use as much or as little of that information as you see fit. This gives you a win-win situation—you have minimal expense and a minimal investment of time on your part, and you can still get valuable insights that can make you money.

Even if your decision is to purchase ready-made astro-trading indicators from a reputable financial astrologer and then add them to your own personal trading mix, you may find it helpful to consult with a knowledgeable coach on a short-term basis, just to make sure that you've got your feet on the ground as you start to engage with the unique insights that financial astrology can provide.

But no matter which of these alternatives is right for you, there are some very valuable resources available for you to use as you explore financial astrology or work towards personal astro-trading mastery.

In addition to my own personal work as a trader, a writer, and a market researcher, I'm also a professionally certified astrologer, with the highest credentials obtainable from the American Federation of Astrologers, the National Council on Geocosmic Research, and the International Society for Astrological Research. In that capacity I regularly work with clients in developing their personal and financial strategies, and I work with active traders as well, providing them with personal coaching and mentoring services to improve their skills as astro-traders. That's why I'm particularly tuned in to the tools and resources that are available for you, especially if you are unfamiliar with the principles of astro-trading and if the goal is to help you the most as you begin your discovery of financial astrology.

First of all, I strongly suggest that you take a look at the astro-trading membership website at http://www.FinancialCyclesWeekly.com. This web site is loaded with all kinds of free resources that will answer your questions about financial astrology and give you lots of first-hand information about how financial astrology can help you make money in the markets by using astro-trading methodologies.

If you're interested in getting a more comprehensive view of the basics of financial astrology, you may also want to investigate my

Basic Stock Market Astrology Home Study Course, which you can find online for ordering at http://www.BasicMarketCourse.com. This is a complete study program, equivalent to a college-level introductory course in all the basics of using astrology in the stock market. It features more than 30 hours of audio instruction, plus more than 250 pages of handouts and exercise materials, along with a bonus DVD featuring an update on some of the latest advances in this exciting field.

You'll want to consider the *Basic Stock Market Astrology Home Study Course* whether you just want to get a complete overview of financial astrology and then start using it in your personal approach to the markets, or whether you are serious about learning all you can about financial astrology and have set your sites on mastering all the knowledge it takes to become a financial astrologer yourself. Either way, the *Basic Stock Market Astrology Home Study Course* will give you a solid foundation in an easy-to-follow format that you can use to learn at your own pace. And one of the best things about this course is that it gives you specific guidance on how to keep your money safe as you learn the secrets of astro-trading and of applying financial astrology to the markets.

Finally, let me also suggest some of the enhancements to my weekly email newsletter, *FinancialCyclesWeekly*, that are available to you through the membership programs on the website at http://www.FinancialCyclesWeekly.com. I write and distribute this weekly newsletter to traders, students of financial astrology, and other readers throughout the world who subscribe to membership services through the website.

No matter what level of involvement in financial astrology is right for you, I'm confident that you'll find something of value in *FinancialCyclesWeekly* newsletter. It can augment your studies if you're serious about learning financial astrology for yourself. But actually, this newsletter does a lot more than that.

It's the ideal solution for you if you want to profit from financial astrology, but if you don't have the time or the inclination to go through an extensive learning process for yourself, preferring instead to apply a few specific astro-trading skills and trade equities profitably.

FinancialCyclesWeekly newsletter provides you with the key information you need in order to start profiting from a weekly astro-trading plan. By using the information in the newsletter you can craft a specific plan that matches your personal needs while providing you with consistent opportunities to analyze market positions strategically.

While you'll find plenty of information in this newsletter that will be helpful to you if you want to understand how financial astrology really works, its main emphasis is on practical, real-world information that can help you use financial astrology to make money in the markets right away!

In each issue, you'll find reviews of the current trends in the major market indices, along with forecasts for the precious metals markets as well. On top of that, each issue of *FinancialCyclesWeekly* features specific weekly "Stocks to Watch", along with a Model Portfolio that includes key money management information to help you protect your investment capital.

After all, in keeping with Billionaire Strategy #8, even though trading in stocks inevitably involves some losses as well as gains, the most important thing for you to do is to hold on to the money you've already got by keeping those losses small while you push those gains to greater and greater heights. In the newsletter you'll find exact stop-loss levels for each active market position, guiding your trade management to produce minimum losses and maximum regular profits.

By the way, the Model Portfolio in *FinancialCyclesWeekly* has a great track record in outperforming the major market averages. During the past nine years, it has consistently outperformed the S&P 500 index, and has brought in profits averaging more than 35% each year.

If you're sincerely interested in moving toward billionaire status, this is important, practical information you definitely will want to get regularly. *FinancialCyclesWeekly* is a paid membership subscription that goes out to readers throughout the world by email at the start of each trading week. When it arrives in your email inbox, you can spend as little as 15 or 20 minutes reviewing the key steps you need to take to set up a couple of stock trades for the week, to make adjustments to your portfolio positions and protect your investment capital, and flag ideas for further consideration. With a minimal amount of time and effort on your part, you'll be gaining the insights of professional financial astrology, ready to help you make money in the markets—and you'll be a part of an exclusive group of people in the know, people who are dedicated to profiting from the money-making magic of the astro-trading approach to putting the 8 Billionaire Strategies to work.

You'll find samples and complete details about FinancialCyclesWeekly on the website at http://www.FinancialCyclesWeekly.com. When you go there, be sure to take a look at some of the money-saving introductory subscription offers that are available. If you're not already a subscribing member, the best way for you to understand what this newsletter can do for you is to get a few issues for yourself—there are very inexpensive ways of doing that, to make sure that there is little or no financial risk to you.

When you read the newsletter for a few weeks, when you personally track the stock recommendations and take a look at the week-to-week performance of the Financial Cycles Model Portfolio, then I'm sure you'll begin to understand what the astro-trading edge can do for your financial well-being.

The Words of a Billionaire

Thanks for taking the time to read this little book. In it I've tried to give you a concise introduction to some billionaire thinking that you can put to practical use to improve the results you're getting in the markets.

As a part of my personal quest for deeper understanding of billionaires' secrets and strategies, financial astrology has truly changed my life in profound and profitable ways. And I firmly believe you can have the same kind of experience, especially if you sincerely want to join the growing ranks of the world's great billionaires.

As you apply the 8 Billionaire Strategies in your own life and trading, please remember the big benefits that financial astrology can bring to you:

It will help you identify big opportunities ahead of time so that you can be ready to take full advantage of them when they occur.

It will enhance your timing for short-term trading to create more profitable outcomes.

It will give you a much better understanding of long-term cycles and how they work, so you can take more appropriate risks.

It will help you understand yourself more completely, both as a person and as a trader active in the markets.

It will help you align your risk-taking activities with the natural flow, so that you can move more effortlessly in and out of the markets in safe and profitable ways.

It will improve the quality of your market analysis and your market forecasting.

It will open your mind to new, surprising possibilities, possibilities for enhancing your wealth, possibilities for expanding your own personal potential, and possibilities for richer, more fulfilling discoveries in the world around you.

And above all, financial astrology and the application of astro-trading techniques will help you make more money.

When it comes to making money, I don't think we can find a more appropriate example than the billionaires of the world. Earlier I mentioned J. P. Morgan, America's first billionaire, and his use of astrology. He was quite a remarkable individual, a man who had a huge personal impact on the country, on the world, and on the future of finance. And it was J. P. Morgan who reputedly once said that "Millionaires don't use astrology. Billionaires do!"

That's quite a remarkable statement.

"Millionaires don't use astrology. Billionaires do!"

I don't think I could have said it better myself. And as far as I'm concerned, it IS the billionaire's secret, the most effective and consistent way of following all eight of the Billionaire Strategies we have discussed in this book.

So if becoming a billionaire is one of the personal dreams that you want to see become a reality, be sure to keep this billionaire's secret in mind. Remember the reasons for exploring financial astrology yourself.

Better yet, do what billionaires do by putting ideas into action. Make sure you take time right now to follow up on this important information. Please don't put it off! Taking action right away can make a big difference in your financial future. In fact, it can be the key to your success no matter what your goals are.

Whether or not you're ready to see yourself enjoying life as one of the world's next billionaires, the simple fact that you have this book in your hands means that you've taken the first step toward better, more abundant results in your trading and in your life. If you listen closely, I'm sure you can hear destiny knocking at your door. It's waiting for you to grab the opportunity of the present moment, to hang on to it with all your might and run with is as far as you can see, as the theme music for your personal championship rings in your ears. All that's needed is for you to make the first move.

So don't delay any longer. Take a moment right now, go to your computer, and log on to http://www.FinancialCyclesWeekly.com. Explore all the information and free resources that are waiting for you there. And while you're at it, pay a visit to http://www.BasicMarketCourse.com as well. Or just do an online search for "astro-trading" and take a look at the websites that come up.

But no matter what you do, get started right away. At the very least, take the time to look around, to see what's available and discover what opportunities best match your interests, experience, and personal learning style.

Then, if you decide that you're personally ready to begin profiting from the astro-trading advantage yourself, you may want to consider working with an astro-trading coach or mentor. If you do, keep these five guidelines in mind:

First of all, make sure your astro-trading coach has solid astrological experience as well as practical experience in the markets. Unfortunately there are all sorts of people who call themselves astrologers, and they have a wide range of competency and personal integrity. It's best to look for an astrologer who has professional certification from recognized organizations like the AFA, NCGR, or ISAR.

Second, find a coach or a mentor who will help you focus on your individual strengths and weaknesses in crafting a trading plan that's customized for you, rather than simply giving you astrological market indicators or prefabricated trading systems. Remember that effective training in astro-trading must include attention to the market, the trade, and the trader as well.

Third, make sure that your coach has knowledge of and access to state-of-the-art astro-trading tools, and can give you some guidance in putting those tools to work.

Fourth, ask your mentor to guide you in effective money management skills if you haven't already mastered them yourself. You can't make money in the markets if you aren't participating in the markets, and you can't participate in the markets if you've lost all your trading capital. Look to your coach to help you keep that from happening.

Finally, in working with a coach or mentor, make sure that you do most of the work yourself. While your mentor should be able to give you lots of solid advice and help you find answers to your most pressing questions, you will get the greatest benefit from the coaching relationship if you're clear about applying the principles you are learning as rapidly as possible. Be prepared to take action and make mistakes, because it's exactly that kind of experience that will anchor the knowledge more firmly in your consciousness and help you become more confident in applying it for profits in the markets. Don't count on your coach to do the work for you!

Above all, I want to encourage you to pursue the Billionaire Strategies right away. They are reliable guideposts that will serve you well, and you will find them coming to life in your own experience much more vividly if you add financial astrology and astro-trading principles to your pursuit.

That's true whether you decide to become a financial astrologer yourself, whether you want learn just enough about financial astrology to be able to combine it with other market strategies, or whether you simply want to profit from the end results, from the insights that professional financial astrology can offer about today's markets and tomorrow's trading opportunities.

Good luck with your trading!

A Free Bonus for You

Because you have this book, you are entitled to a FREE Astro-Trading Strategy Session! Whether or not you are currently using astrology in your trading, you'll profit form this one-on-one intensive evaluation of your trading practices and results.

It's a $1,200 value, yours free at:

bit.ly/StrategyBonus

CPSIA information can be obtained
at www.ICGtesting.com
Printed in the USA
LVOW04s1451060316
477992LV00029B/1051/P

9 781933 198286